a book about

WHAT AUTISM CAN BE LIKE

Written and illustrated by

Sue Adams

Foreword by Donna Williams

Jessica Kingsley Publishers
London and Philadelphia

First published in 2009
by Jessica Kingsley Publishers
116 Pentonville Road
London N1 9JB, UK
and
400 Market Street, Suite 400
Philadelphia, PA 19106, USA

www.jkp.com

Copyright © Sue Adams 2009
Foreword copyright © Donna Williams 2009
Printed digitally since 2010

Library of Congress Cataloging in Publication Data

Adams, Sue.
A book about what autism can be like / Sue Adams ; foreword by Donna Williams.
p. cm.
ISBN 978-1-84310-940-2 (pb : alk. paper)
1. Autism--Juvenile literature. 2. Autistic children--Juvenile literature. I. Title.
RC553.A88A334 2008
616.85'882--dc22
2008024650

British Library Cataloguing in Publication Data

A CIP catalogue record for this book is available from the British Library

ISBN 978 1 84310 940 2

This book is dedicated to my real life Christopher,
to his brothers Peter and Benjamin and my husband Russell.
Special children teach adults to become special parents.

Thank you to Shelley, Marg and Ellie
for being in Chris's story.

Foreword

Mid to late childhood is a time when children start to become aware of their similarities and differences. For children with Autism Spectrum Disorder (ASD) this can be a time of awakening, a turning point where they may sink or swim. Sometimes this direction is strongly influenced by the way other children understand their own differences in the wider context of those with ASD. Sue Adams' book, *A Book About What Autism Can be Like*, will be of help to children struggling to see diversity and difference in a positive light and aid teachers, siblings, those with ASD and their classmates.

Donna Williams, Dip Ed, BA (Hons)
author of Autism: An Inside Out Approach

This is Chris and Andrew.
Chris and Andrew go to school.

Chris and Andrew have many
things the same.

Chris and Andrew have many
things different.

Chris and Andrew sometimes think
about the same things.

But they sometimes think about
the same things in different ways.

Chris often thinks differently
because he has autism. This is not
a problem, it is just different.

Think how boring it would be if we
all thought the same!

People with autism can get overloaded when too much happens for their brain to cope with all at the same time.

A room filled with lots of posters
and decorations may look exciting
to Andrew. But it is difficult for
Chris to take in all of those things
at the same time.

When the teacher says "Stop!"
Andrew's brain hears the message
and tells Andrew to stop.

When Chris's brain hears the
teacher say "Stop!" it also hears
many extra messages.

Chris's brain has trouble working out which message to listen to first. This can make it look like Chris is not listening at all.

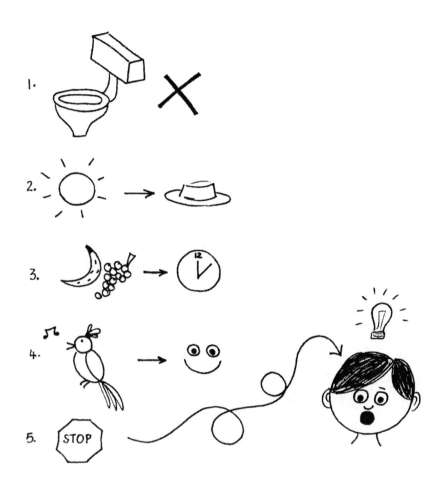

But then the messages get processed (this means working out what the messages mean, like a computer does)...

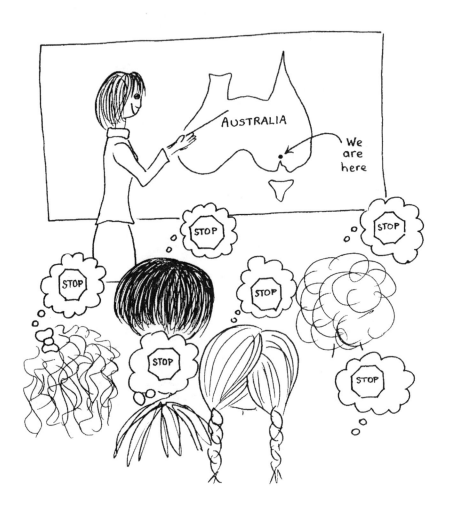

...and Chris can do as the
messages say.

Sometimes friends can help by gently explaining to Chris what the teacher said.

Chris may need to be told in a
different way. This does not
mean repeating the same thing
or saying it LOUDER.

Instead of telling him, it might be
helpful to show him.

Chris can think more clearly if he draws his thoughts to keep track of them. Or he might use objects or gestures (hand signals).

This doesn't mean he is busy
playing. It just helps to make his
thinking real to him.

Sometimes Chris seems to "shut down" when too much information comes his way. He ignores the world until the information rush slows down. Chris needs to think of one thing at a time.

This is when he needs some quiet
time for his brain to catch up.
Quiet time is when you sit by
yourself to become calm. It does
not mean you are in trouble. It
is like quiet thinking time.

Chris's classmates understand that autism makes it difficult for Chris to make friends. Even when Chris likes someone, he does not always know what words to say to them.

At school, it can help Chris to work
at a table on his own sometimes.
He joins in group activities at
other times.

Andrew helps when Chris looks sad
or confused. He understands that
Chris is just different. It is not a
problem. He gets to know what can
help Chris to calm down.

Like when Chris rocks or makes his
own special humming noises to
comfort himself.

Or when he likes to be in the dark.

People sense the world around them through five senses. These are: smelling, tasting, touching, seeing and hearing.

Autism can make these senses
really **STRONG** or very weak.

Chris has very strong senses.
Andrew doesn't notice the buzzing
noise that the light tubes make.
But Chris hears it really loudly.

Touching is hard to do sometimes.
Chris needs to say "Hi" and wave
instead of hugging or shaking
hands. It is not because he does
not like the other person.

Some people with autism really
like bright flashing lights.
Others find bright lights painful
to their eyes.

Even people with autism are
different from each other!

Lots of famous people in history
are thought to have had autism.
Edison the inventor, Einstein
the scientist...

...and Mozart the composer. Their
ideas were so amazing because
they were VERY different from
everyone else.

Sometimes answers to the teacher's question rush into Chris's brain. He has to say them quickly before something else crowds in.

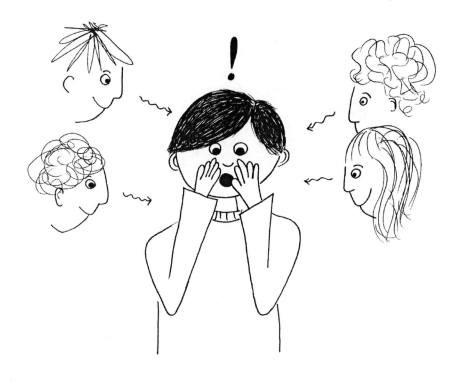

He doesn't mean to take someone else's turn. But his classmates understand that.

At other times, Chris's autism
means he takes longer than
Andrew to think of an answer
to a question...

...but the answer can be really
amazing when his brain finally
works it out!

Nobody really knows why people have autism. But lots of boys and girls have it.

We do know you cannot catch
autism from someone else.

Chris's classmates know that
things sometimes upset him. And
maybe the upsetting things are not
the same as they were yesterday.

But they also know that Chris has a great sense of humour. Different people find different things funny!

When someone is different
from you, you just need to get
to know them. Getting to know
people is fantastic.

So being different is actually
pretty cool!

Lightning Source UK Ltd.
Milton Keynes UK
UKOW032045050413

208746UK00001B/2/P